What's in a
Pond?

by Martha E. H. Rustad

CAPSTONE PRESS
a capstone imprint

Little Pebble is published by Capstone Press,
1710 Roe Crest Drive, North Mankato, Minnesota 56003
www.capstonepub.com

Library of Congress Cataloging-in-Publication Data
Rustad, Martha E. H. (Martha Elizabeth Hillman), 1975– author.
 What's in a pond? / by Martha E. H. Rustad.
    pages cm.—(Little pebble. What's in there?)
 Summary: "Simple nonfiction text and full-color photographs present
animals and plants found in a pond"—Provided by the publisher.
 Audience: Ages 5–7 Audience: K to grade 3
 Includes bibliographical references and index.
  ISBN 978-1-4914-6010-8 (library binding)
  ISBN 978-1-4914-6022-1 (pbk.)
  ISBN 978-1-4914-6034-4 (ebook pdf)
1. Pond animals—Juvenile literature. 2. Ponds—Juvenile literature. I. Title.
II. Title: What is in a pond?
 QL146.3.R87 2016
 591.763'6—dc23   2015001937

For Kashif, Kaiyaan, Kamran, and Khalil.—MEHR

Editorial Credits
Erika L. Shores, editor; Cynthia Della-Rovere, designer; Svetlana Zhurkin, media researcher;
Katy LaVigne, production specialist

Photo Credits
Alamy: Marvin Dembinsky Photo Associates, 5; iStockphoto: Michelinedesgroseilliers, 17;
Newscom: Photoshot/NHPA/Stephen Krasemann, 21; Shutterstock: CCat82, 9 (back), Dan
Mensinger, 7 (inset), Dirk Ercken, 3, Eric Isselee, back cover, 8, Ian Grainger, 10, Iliuta Goean,
13, Josef Bosak, 15, Karen Hermann, 7 (back), MyImages Micha, 11, panbazil, 4, perlphoto, 9
(inset), rolfik, 1, 14, Tea Maeklong, 6, 12, 20, Vetapi, 18—19, Yuriy Kulik, cover

Printed in China
042015 008832LEOF15

Table of Contents

At the Pond 4

Pond Plants. 6

Pond Animals 10

Glossary 22
Read More . . . 23
Internet Sites . 23
Index 24

At the Pond

Find a pond.

Look around!

What lives here?

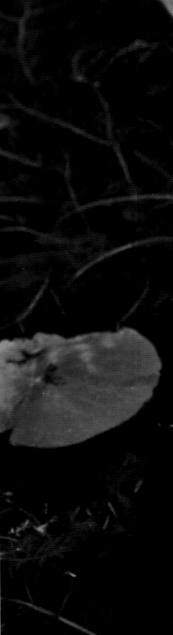

Pond Plants

Look!

Tiny algae float in ponds.

They make rocks slippery.

algae

Reeds stand tall.

Lily pads float.

reeds

lily pad

Pond Animals

Tadpoles swim.

They grow into frogs.

tadpoles

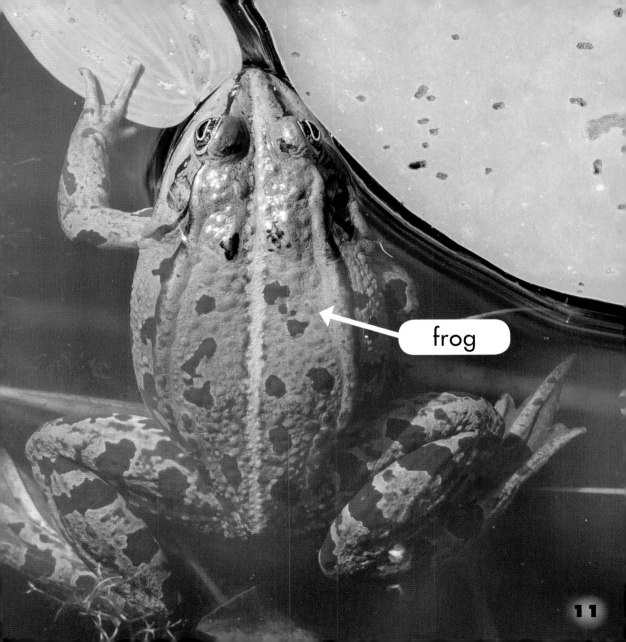

frog

Dragonflies fly low.

They munch flying bugs.

13

Snap!

A turtle nabs a fish.

Shy turtles hide.

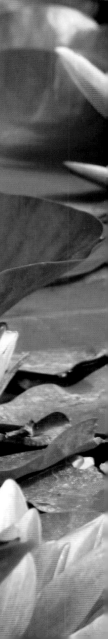

Swish!

Tiny minnows dart.

They lay eggs at
the bottom.

17

Quack!

Baby ducks follow mom.

She teaches them to swim.

19

A beaver cuts down a tree.

He builds a dam.

It makes a pond.

Ponds make good homes.

Glossary

algae—tiny floating plants

dam—a barrier built in a stream by a beaver

minnow—a small fish

reed—a tall, thin plant that grows in wetlands, marshes, and ponds

tadpole—a young frog; tadpoles look like fish

Read More

Leake, Diyan. *Ponds.* Water, Water Everywhere! Chicago: Heinemann, 2015.

West, David. *Pond Life.* Nora the Naturalist's Animals. Mankato, Minn.: Smart Apple Media, 2014.

Worth, Bonnie. *Would You Rather Be a Pollywog?: All About Pond Life.* New York: Random House, 2010.

Internet Sites

FactHound offers a safe, fun way to find Internet sites related to this book. All of the sites on FactHound have been researched by our staff.

Here's all you do:
Visit *www.facthound.com*
Type in this code: 9781491460108

Super-cool stuff! Check out projects, games and lots more at **www.capstonekids.com**

Index

algae, 6

beavers, 20
bugs, 12

dams, 20
dragonflies, 12
ducks, 18

eggs, 16

fish, 14
frogs, 10

lily pads, 8

minnows, 16

reeds, 8
rocks, 6

tadpoles, 10
turtles, 14

3 1125 00990 9126